Supplement to
A Digest of Supreme Court Decisions Affecting Education

by
Perry A. Zirkel

A publication from Phi Delta Kappa
Bloomington, Indiana

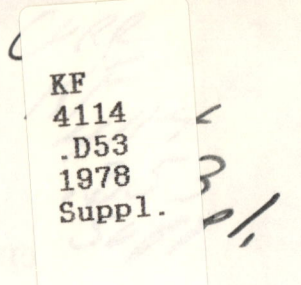

Cover design by Kathe Swann

©1982 Phi Delta Kappa
All rights reserved
Library of Congress Catalogue Card Number LC 81-86629
ISBN 0-87367-426-X
Printed in the United States of America

To Carol
This one is totally for,
and partially with, you.

Acknowledgements

I wish to express my appreciation to Phi Delta Kappa International, under the able leadership of executive secretary Lowell C. Rose, for the encouragement to undertake this supplement to *A Digest of Supreme Court Decisions Affecting Education*. Further, I wish to acknowledge with enthusiastic esteem the editorial guidance of Derek L. Burleson, editor of Special Publications at Phi Delta Kappa. Finally, my angelic secretary Sharon Yaszewski, my patient wife Carol, and my precious children Jessica and Seth all deserve a public thank you.

Table of Contents

	Page
Introduction	vii

Chapter I. School Board Elections and Liability

Monell v. Department of Social Services	4	1
Owen v. City of Independence, Missouri	4	1
Mobile v. Bolden	1	2
Maine v. Thiboutot	4	3
Interim Board of Trustees v. Coalition to Preserve Houston	*1	4
City of Newport v. Fact Concerts	4	5

Chapter II. Church-State Relationships in Education

New York v. Cathedral Academy	2	6
NLRB v. Catholic Bishop of Chicago...............	2	7
Stone v. Graham	1	7
St. Martin Evangelical Lutheran Church v. South Dakota	2	8
Beggans v. Public Funds for Public Schools of New Jersey.....................................	*1	9
Committee for Public Education v. Regan	2	9

Chapter III. Student Rights and Responsibilities

Idaho Department of Employment v. Smith	1	11
Board of Curators v. Horowitz	3	11
Carey v. Piphus	1	12
Regents of the University of California v. Bakke	3 (cr)	29
Cannon v. University of Chicago...................	3	13
Southeastern Community College v. Davis	3	14
University of Texas v. Camenisch	3 (cr)	34

v

Chapter IV. Employee Rights and Responsibilities

Nashville Gas Co. v. Satty	4	16
United States v. South Carolina	*1	17
Los Angeles v. Manhart	4	18
Board of Trustees of Keene State College v. Sweeney	3	18
Givhan v. Western Line Consolidated School District	1	19
Harrah Independent School District v. Martin	1	20
Ambach v. Norwick	1	21
United Steelworkers v. Weber	4	22
Gomez v. Toledo	*4	23
Maine v. Thiboutot	4 (cr)	3
Delaware State College v. Ricks	3	24
EEOC v. Associated Dry Goods Corp.	4	25
Texas Department of Community Affairs v. Burdine	4	25
Northwest Airlines v. Transport Workers Union	4	27
County of Washington v. Gunther	4	27
City of Newport v. Fact Concerts	4 (cr)	5

Chapter V. Race, Language, and Sex Discrimination

Nashville Gas Co. v. Satty	4 (cr)	16
United States v. South Carolina	*1 (cr)	17
Los Angeles v. Manhart	4 (cr)	18
Regents of the University of California v. Bakke	3	29
Board of Trustees of Keene State College v. Sweeney	3 (cr)	18
United Steelworkers v. Weber	4 (cr)	22
Columbus Board of Education v. Penick	1	30
Board of Education of New York City v. Harris	1	31
Dayton Board of Education v. Brinkman ("Dayton II")	1	31
Mobile v. Bolden	1 (cr)	2
Armour v. Nix	*1	33
Delaware State College v. Ricks	3 (cr)	24
EEOC v. Associated Dry Goods Corp.	4 (cr)	25
Interim Board of Trustees v. Coalition to Preserve Houston	1 (cr)	4
Texas Department of Community Affairs v. Burdine	4 (cr)	25
Northwest Airlines v. Transport Workers Union	4 (cr)	27
County of Washington v. Gunther	4 (cr)	27

Chapter VI. Procedural Parameters

University of Texas v. Camenisch	3	34
Table of Cases		35
Index		37

Introduction

This supplement provides a four-year update to *A Digest of Supreme Court Decisions Affecting Education* published by Phi Delta Kappa in 1978, and thus includes cases decided by the Court between August 1977 and August 1981. The *Digest,* which I edited, was a project of the Phi Delta Kappa Commission on the Impact of Court Decisions. The research and writing of this supplement, however, is solely my responsibility.

The criteria for selecting the cases to include in this supplement are the same as for the original *Digest:* namely, Supreme Court decisions directly affecting elementary and secondary education. Cases that do not seem readily to meet these criteria are not included, notwithstanding their related importance in higher education (e.g., *Elkins v. Moreno,* 435 U.S. 647 (1978); *Yeshiva University v. National Labor Relations Board,* 444 U.S. 673 (1978); and in other institutional contexts (e.g., *Parham v. J.R.,* 442 U.S. 584 (1979); *Secretary of Public Welfare of Pennsylvania v. Institutionalized Juveniles,* 442 U.S. 640 (1979); *Pennhurst State School and Hospital v. Halderman,* 101 S. Ct. 1537 (1981)).

As in the original *Digest,* the categories of litigants are coded to the right of the case entries in the Table of Contents as follows: 1—public school, 2—private school, 3—higher education, and 4—non school. The organization of the chapters follows that of the original *Digest,* except for a modification of the first chapter to reflect the increasingly important "liability" issue. The final, procedural chapter has been retained; but vacated and dismissed decisions have been discontinued. The Table of Contents indicates cross references (cr) for cases that fit more than one chapter heading; also summary affirmances are indicated by an asterisk (*).

The format for each case entry follows that of the *Digest:* the citation, the facts, the holding, and the basis for the decision. The citations follow the style of the Harvard Law Review Association, *A Uniform System of Citation,* 12th ed. (1976). The volume number and the first page of the case as it appears in the official reports of the Supreme Court (U.S. for *United States Reports*) are given, except where only an unofficial publication of the decision ("S.Ct." for West's *Supreme Court Reporter*) was available at the time this digest was completed in September 1981. The lower court history of the decisions is not listed, except in cases resulting in a summary affirmance. For the typical case, the form of the citation is summarized below:

MOBILE v. BOLDEN   446   U.S.   55   1980
(appellant)   (appellee)   (vol.#)   (U.S. Reports) (page#) (year of decision)

The facts for each decision are presented as much as possible in lay language. For the sake of brevity, facts not essential to the decision are not included in the summary. The "holding" is extrapolated from the majority opinion of the Court except for summary affirmances, in which instances the facts and decision of the lower court are summarized. The vote of the Court is reported as follows: number of justices in the majority, number in the concurrence, followed by the number dissenting, indicated, for example, by (5/2 x 2). The numbers are arbitrarily listed as one-half in some cases as an approximate indication of split votes as follows: (5/2½ x 1½). Reference to cases in the original *Digest* are indicated by (*supra m.v.*), meaning main volume.

The basis for each decision is listed in terms of the constitutional provisions, statutory sections, or judicial precedents cited by the Court as its primary authority. Legal reasoning is presented only to the extent it helps establish the authority for the decisions. The basis for cases resulting in a summary affirmance is given, in the absence of a readily available alternative, in terms of the lower court's opinion. A Table of Cases and an Index complete the supplement.

Thus, this supplement is designed to complement the coverage of the original *Digest,* published in 1978, so as to keep educators and others up to date on the increasing impact of the Supreme Court on education.

Perry A. Zirkel
Bethlehem, Pennsylvania
September 1981

I. School Board Elections and Liability

MONELL v. DEPARTMENT OF SOCIAL SERVICES, 436 U.S. 658 (1978)*

Facts: Female employees of the Department of Social Services and the Board of Education of New York City brought this class action against the department and its commissioner, the board and its chancellor, and the city and its mayor under 42 U.S.C. § 1983, which provides that every "person" who under color of state law deprives any other person of any federally protected rights, privileges, or immunities shall be civilly liable to the injured party. The individual defendants were sued solely in their official capacities. The essence of the complaint was that the Department and the Board had, as a matter of official policy, compelled pregnant employees to take unpaid leaves of absence before such leaves were required for medical reasons.

Holding: (6/1x2) Local governing bodies (including school boards) and their officials sued in their official capacities are "persons" within the meaning of 42 U.S.C. § 1983, except that they cannot be held liable under § 1983 on a respondent superior theory, i.e., for an injury inflicted solely by their employees or agents.

Basis: Re-examining the language and legislative history of the Civil Rights Act, now codified as 42 U.S.C. § 1983, the Court reversed its prior ruling in *Monroe v. Pape,* 365 U.S. 167 (1961) insofar as it held that local governments are wholly immune from § 1983 suits.

OWEN v. CITY OF INDEPENDENCE, MISSOURI, 445 U.S. 622 (1980)

Facts: Plaintiff was appointed in 1967 to an indefinite term as chief of police by the then city manager. In 1972 the plaintiff and a new city manager engaged in a dispute over plaintiff's administration of the police department's property room. The city manager conducted an investigation, which found record keeping

---

*For a case vacated in light of this decision, see *Kornit v. Board of Education,* 438 U.S. 902 (1978).

problems but no criminal violations. On April 10 of that year, the manager asked plaintiff to resign and accept another position in the police department, warning that he would be terminated if he refused. On April 13 the city manager issued a public statement reporting the results of the investigation and assuring that steps had been initiated to correct the discrepancies in the administration of the property room. Plaintiff, having consulted with counsel, formally requested written notice of the charges and a public hearing to respond to them. Although his request received no immediate response, the city council soon thereafter voted that the investigative reports be released to the news media and to the prosecutor, and that the city manager take appropriate action against the plaintiff. The city manager discharged him the very next day. No reason was given for the dismissal; plaintiff only received a brief written notice stating that the dismissal was made pursuant to a specified provision of the city charter. His earlier demand for a specification of charges and a public hearing was ignored, and a subsequent request for an appeal of the discharge decision was denied. He brought suit under § 1983 for violation of his due process rights.

Holding: (5x4) The qualified immunity of local governmental officials and agents does not extend to local governing bodies (e.g., a municipal corporation) as a defense to liability under § 1983.

Basis: The language of Section 1983 and its legislative history are expansive. The Court has only found immunities in contexts where there is a tradition of immunity strongly rooted in the common law and supported by strong policy reasons. There is not a tradition of, nor policy support for, immunity for municipal corporations.

MOBILE v. BOLDEN, 446 U.S. 55 (1980)

Facts: Mobile, Alabama, is governed by a commission consisting of three members elected by the voters of the city at large. A group of black residents of Mobile brought a class action alleging, among other things, that the practice of electing the city commissioners at large unfairly diluted the voting strength of blacks in violation of the Fourteenth and Fifteenth Amendments. The district court found that blacks in Mobile register and vote without hindrance.

Holding: (4/2x3) An at-large system of electing a municipal body does not violate Amendments Fourteen or Fifteen unless there is a showing of purposeful racial discrimination.

Basis: Racially discriminatory motivation is a necessary ingredient of a Fifteenth Amendment violation. Similarly, only if there is purposeful discrimination can there be a violation of the Fourteenth Amendment's equal protection clause, and this principle applies to claims of racial discrimination affecting voting just as it does to other claims of unconstitutional conduct. Since Mobile is a unitary electoral district and the commission elections are conducted at large, there is no violation of the one person, one vote principle. Disproportionate impact alone is insufficient to establish a claim of unconstitutional racial vote dilution.

MAINE v. THIBOUTOT, 448 U.S. 1 (1980)

Facts: Plaintiffs are a married couple who have eight children, three by the husband's previous marriage. The Maine Department of Human Services notified him that, in computing the welfare benefits to which he was entitled for the three children exclusively his, it would no longer allow support for the other five children, even though he was legally obligated to support them. After exhausting their administrative remedies, plaintiffs brought suit in state court, challenging the state's interpretation of the federal Social Security Act and claiming relief under § 1983 for themselves and others similarly situated. Section 1983 established liability of any person who under color of state law deprives another person of "any rights, privileges, or immunities secured by the Constitution *and laws*" [emphasis supplied]. Attorney's fee awards are possible in such actions under § 1988.

Holding: (6x3) Sections 1983 and 1988 apply to violations of federal statutes as well as the federal Constitution.

Basis: Given that Congress attached no modifiers to the phrase "and laws," the plain language of § 1983 undoubtedly embraces plaintiffs' claim that the defendants violated a federal statute. Even if the language were ambiguous, several of the Court's previous decisions (e.g., *Monell* and *Owen supra*), have suggested explicitly or implicitly that the § 1983 remedy broadly encompasses violations of federal statutory as well as a constitutional law. The legislative history is limited but not inconsistent with this interpretation. The plain language and legislative history of § 1988 (the Civil Rights Attorney's Fees Awards Act) similarly supports its applicability to deprivations of statutory rights, whether brought in state or federal courts.

INTERIM BOARD OF TRUSTEES OF WESTHEIMER INDEPENDENT SCHOOL DISTRICT v. COALITION TO PRESERVE HOUSTON, 494 F. Supp. 738 (S.D. Tex. 1980), *aff'd,* **101 S. Ct. 1335 (1981)**

Facts: Section 5 of the amended Voting Rights Act of 1965 prohibits a state or political subdivision from establishing any voting qualification or procedure different from that in effect on November 1, 1972, without obtaining prior approval from the Attorney General or the federal district court for the District of Columbia. The proposed change must not have the purpose or effect of abridging the right to vote on account of race, color, or language. The interim board of Westheimer Independent School District requested the Attorney General to grant advance approval for a special election scheduled for January 15, 1977. On January 13, 1977, he denied approval. An ad hoc coalition filed suit on January 14 to enjoin the election, but their request to convene a three-judge court was denied, and the election was held as scheduled. The coalition's case was consolidated with similar suits, and a three-judge court ruled that school districts in Texas are covered by the Act and thus should be enjoined from conducting elections under changed voting procedures until obtaining the required approval.

Decision: (9x0) Summarily affirmed

Holding: (of the lower court) 1) Where a school board election is held in deliberate defiance of Section 5 of the Voting Rights Act, the election should be set aside. 2) Plaintiff coalition, as the prevailing party in a Voting Rights Act case, is entitled to an award of reasonable attorney's fees recoverable against the school district, not against the state of Texas nor the Texas Education agency.

Bases: (of the lower court's decision) 1) In previous cases, the Court indicated that among the considerations in determining whether to set aside such elections is whether it was clear at the time of the election that the changes were covered by Section 5. Here the defendant district attempted to have the voting change approved, indicating its awareness of coverage. 2) The coalition meets the "prevailing party" requirement, since it succeeded on the significant issues in the litigation and achieved the benefits sought in bringing the suit. The award is not recoverable against the state of Texas or its education agency because, under Texas law, local school districts are not sufficiently identified with and controlled by the state. The tradition of local control of education is long and strong in Texas, as reflected in the express limitations on the legislature's power to statutorily control local school districts.

CITY OF NEWPORT v. FACT CONCERTS, 101 S. Ct. 2748 (1981)

Facts: A corporation organized for the purpose of promoting musical concerts sought to obtain a license from the city of Newport, Rhode Island, to present the city's 1975 jazz festival. The contract gave the plaintiff-corporation control over the choice of performers and type of music to be played, and it granted the defendant-city the right to cancel the license without liability if "in the opinion of the City the interests of public safety demand." Shortly before the concert, the corporation hired the group Blood, Sweat, and Tears as a replacement for a previously engaged performer who was unable to appear. Members of the city council, including the mayor, attempted to cancel the contract because they felt that the above mentioned group was a rock rather than jazz band; and the city had experienced crowd disturbances at previous rock concerts. Plaintiff-organization obtained a restraining order in state court, and the two-day concert was held as scheduled. However, due to adverse publicity, fewer than half the available tickets were sold. The promoters brought suit against the city, the mayor, and six other council members, alleging that the city's cancellation of the license amounted to a violation of their constitutional rights under color of state law. They thus sought compensatory and punitive damages under 42 U.S.C. § 1983. The federal district court in a jury trial awarded them punitive damages ($275,000), in addition to compensatory damages ($72,910), against both the individual officials and the city. The case was appealed.

Holding: (6x3) Local governments (including school boards) are immune from punitive damages under § 1983.

Basis: Citing *Owen* (*supra*), the Court applied a two-part approach, examining common law history and public policy considerations. When Congress enacted what is now § 1983, the immunity of municipality from punitive damages as common law was well established. Similarly, public policy considerations in terms of the objectives of punitive damages and their relationship to the goals of § 1983 do not support exposing a municipality to punitive damages for the bad faith actions of the officials.

II. Church-State Relationships in Education

NEW YORK v. CATHEDRAL ACADEMY, 434 U.S. 125 (1977)*

Facts: In response to *Levitt I* (*supra m.v.*), which declared New York's Mandated Services Act unconstitutional, the New York Legislature statutorily authorized what the district court's injunction, upheld by the Supreme Court, had prohibited: reimbursement to sectarian schools for expenses incurred in performing state-mandated services for the academic year which largely predated the Court's decision. Cathedral Academy brought this action for reimbursement under the new Act.

Holding: (6x3) A state statute that authorizes payments to nonpublic schools for services provided pursuant to legislation determined to be unconstitutional and prior to the date of the Court's determination is also invalid if constitutional and equitable considerations weigh against its effectuation.

Basis: Unlike *Lemon II* (*supra m.v.*), in which the district court enjoined prospective but not retroactive payments, the constitutional invalidity of the New York statute is in the payment itself, not in the process of its administration. New York's special reimbursement act, like its Mandated Services Act, is unconstitutional because it has the primary effect of aiding religion. Even if the reimbursement act contemplates an audit mechanism to resolve the establishment of religion problem, this sort of detailed inquiry violates the excessive entanglement test. Further, even assuming that under *Lemon II* a degree of constitutional infirmity may be tolerated if other equitable considerations predominate, the infringement and reliance here are materially different from *Lemon II*.

---

*For a Supreme Court ruling on another statute related to the same situation, see *Committee for Public Education v. Regan.*

NATIONAL LABOR RELATIONS BOARD v. CATHOLIC BISHOP OF CHICAGO, 440 U.S. 490 (1979)

Facts: The National Labor Relations Board (NLRB) only began to assert jurisdiction over private schools and universities in the 1970s. For parochial schools that meet the NLRB's jurisdictional standards with respect to interstate commerce, its policy has been to decline jurisdiction only when the schools were "completely religious," not just "religious associated." In line with this policy, the NLRB certified unions as bargaining agents for lay teachers at two groups of Catholic high schools. The schools refused to bargain with the unions, challenging the NLRB's exercise of jurisdiction on both statutory and constitutional grounds. NLRB found the schools' refusal to bargain to constitute an unfair labor practice and sought enforcement of its bargaining order.

Holding: (5x4) Schools operated by a church to teach both religious and secular subjects are not under the jurisdiction granted by the National Labor Relations Act, and the NLRB is therefore without authority to issue orders against such schools.

Basis: Citing its previous church-state cases (e.g., *Lemon II supra m.v.*), the Court pointed to the pervasiveness of religious authority in church-operated schools and concluded that the NLRB's exercise of jurisdiction would give rise to various constitutional questions. In such cases, the affirmative intention of Congress needs to be clearly expressed. The Court found no such intention in the legislative history of the Act and thus declined to decide whether such an exercise of the NLRB's jurisdiction violates the guarantees of the religion establishment clause of the First Amendment.

STONE v. GRAHAM, 449 U.S. 39 (1980)

Facts: A Kentucky statute required the posting of a copy of the Ten Commandments, procured with private contributions, on the wall of each public school classroom in the state. The statute further provided that each of the 16×20 inch posters of the Commandments bear a notation in small print stating that the "secular" application of the Ten Commandments is clearly seen as the basis of the fundamental legal code of Western civilization and of the common law of the United States.

Holding: (5x4) A state statute which required the posting of the Ten Commandments in every public school classroom is unconstitutional, notwithstanding that the posted copies are privately contributed and labelled as secular material.

Basis: Alluding to the three-part test that it has developed for determining whether a state statute is permissible under the First Amendment's establishment clause, the Court found the Kentucky statute at issue here not to have a secular purpose and therefore to be unconstitutional. As in *Abington (supra m.v.)*, the Court concluded that "the recitation of a supposed secular purpose cannot blind us to the undeniably religious nature of such material." To distinguish it from *Abington,* this is not a case in which the Ten Commandments are integrated into the school curriculum, where the Bible may be used in an appropriate study of history, civilization, ethics, comparative religion, or the like.

ST. MARTIN EVANGELICAL LUTHERAN CHURCH v. SOUTH DAKOTA, 101 S.Ct. 2142 (1981)

Facts: A church-sponsored elementary Christian day school and a secondary school controlled and supported by the Lutheran Synod both claimed to be exempt from paying their school employees' unemployment compensation taxes. The federal Unemployment Tax Act provides an exemption for "service performed—(1) in the employment of (A) a church or convention or association of churches, or (B) an organization ... which is operated, supervised, controlled, or principally supported by a church or a convention or association of churches...." A previous exemption under the Act for service performed in the employ of a school that is not an institution of higher education was repealed.

Holding: (8/1x0) Elementary and secondary schools that have no separate legal existence from a church or from a convention or association of churches are exempt from federal unemployment compensation taxes.

Basis: The language of the legislation and its history supports an interpretation distinguishing between church schools integrated into a church's structure and those separately incorporated. The matter thus being statutorily settled, it is unnecessary to consider the First Amendment issues raised by the plaintiff.

BEGGANS v. PUBLIC FUNDS FOR PUBLIC SCHOOLS OF NEW JERSEY, 590 F.2d 514 (3d Cir. 1979), *aff'd,* 442 U.S. 907 (1979)

Facts: A New Jersey statute provided that a taxpayer who has dependent children attending nonpublic elementary or secondary schools on a full-time basis may have a personal deduction of $1,000 against gross income for each such child. Various organizations as well as several individual taxpayers sued in federal court, contending that, inasmuch as 95% of the nonpublic elementary and secondary schools in New Jersey are religiously affiliated, the exemption violates the First Amendment's establishment clause.

Decision: (9x0) Summarily affirmed

Holding: (of the lower court) A state statute that provides a tax exemption for children attending nonpublic elementary or secondary schools is unconstitutional.

Basis: (of the lower court's decision) The tax exemption meets the first of the Supreme Court's three standards: the requirement of secular purpose. But it encounters an insurmountable obstacle in the second standard: that the primary effect be neither the advancement nor inhibition of religion. This tax relief plan is on close examination like the one found unconstitutional in *Committee for Public Education* (*supra m.v.*), but unlike the one found constitutional in *Walz* (*supra m.v.*). In view of this conclusion, the third standard—the test of excessive government entanglement—need not be reached.

COMMITTEE FOR PUBLIC EDUCATION v. REGAN, 444 U.S. 646 (1980)*

Facts: After a New York statute that appropriated public funding to reimburse both parochial and secular nonpublic schools for performing various mandated services, including the administration, grading, and reporting of the results of tests, was held to be unconstitutional in *Levitt I* (*supra m.v.*), the New York legislature enacted a new statute providing reimbursement to such schools for performing various testing and reporting services mandated by state law. Unlike the earlier statute, the new

---

*This decision should not be confused with *New York v. Cathedral Academy,* which dealt with a statute enacted to try to provide *retrospective* relief to schools that had relied on the statute held unconstitutional in *Levitt*. This decision, however relates to a statute that attempts to revise *prospectively* the statute held unconstitutional in *Levitt.*

version 1) did not include reimbursement for teacher-made tests, and 2) provided an auditing mechanism to ensure that only the actual costs incurred in providing the covered secular services would be reimbursed.

Holding: (5x4) A state statute that provides for payment to nonpublic schools for the actual costs of administering and grading required state-prepared tests is constitutional.

Basis: *Wolman v. Walter* (*supra m.v.*) controls this case. Although the Ohio statute at issue in *Wolman* is not identical to the New York statute at issue here, the differences are not significant. The state-prepared tests and record keeping/reporting functions meet the secular purpose and effect test (see *Lemon I supra m.v.*); and the statute's fiscal arrangements avoid the excessive entanglement standard. The Court's conscious approach to First Amendment establishment clause cases sacrifices clarity and predictability for flexibility and continuing interaction between the courts and the states.

III. Student Rights and Responsibilities

IDAHO DEPARTMENT OF EMPLOYMENT v. SMITH, 434 U.S. 100 (1977)

Facts: An Idaho statute stated that "no person shall be deemed to be unemployed while he is attending a regular established school, excluding night school...." Plaintiff became ineligible for state unemployment benefits when she enrolled in summer school, attending classes from 7 a.m. to 9 a.m. Her attendance thus did not interfere with her availability for future employment in her usual occupation as a retail clerk.

Holding: (5/1x3) A state statute that denies unemployment benefits to otherwise eligible persons who attend school during the day, but not to otherwise eligible persons who attend night school, is not in violation of the equal protection clause of the Fourteenth Amendment.

Bases: It is rational for the state legislature to conclude that because daytime employment is far more plentiful than night-time work, attending school during daytime hours imposed a greater restriction on obtaining full-time employment than did attending school at night. Moreover, the statutory classification served as a predictable and economical means for determining eligibility for benefits.

BOARD OF CURATORS OF UNIVERSITY OF MISSOURI v. HOROWITZ, 435 U.S. 78 (1978)

Facts: Plaintiff was a student on probation in her final year of medical school. The dean informed her of the faculty's dissatisfaction with her clinical performance and of their recommendation that she be dropped from the school unless she showed a dramatic improvement in her clinical competence, peer and patient relations, personal hygiene, and ability to accept criticism. As an "appeal" to their decision not to permit her to graduate on schedule, she was permitted to take a set of oral and practical examinations. The exams were evaluated unfavorably for the most part by several practicing physicians. Upon receipt of their evaluations, a student/faculty evaluation council affirmed its prior position. Upon receiving reports of her remaining work for the year, the council recommended that she be dropped from the school. The faculty coordinating committee and the dean approved the recommendation and notified the student. She appealed in writing to the university's provost who sustained the school's decision after reviewing the record. Per the school's custom, plaintiff was not allowed a hearing before the council or the committee.

Holding: (5½/2x1½) The dismissal of a student from school for academic reasons does not require a hearing.

Basis: Even assuming that plaintiff was deprived of a liberty or property interest, she was accorded at least as much due process as the Fourteenth Amendment requires. A long line of court decisions agree that academic evaluations of a student, in contrast to their disciplinary dismissals, are not amenable to the fact-finding process of judicial and administrative decision making.

CAREY v. PIPHUS, 435 U.S. 247 (1978)*

Facts: The two plaintiffs were a ninth-grade student and a sixth-grade student attending public school in Chicago. Each had been suspended for 20 days, the ninth grader for smoking marijuana during school hours on school property and the sixth grader for wearing an earring in violation of a school rule intended to discourage street gang activities in school. The district court held that both students had been suspended in violation of the Fourteenth Amendment. It also held that school officials were not entitled to qualified immunity from damages under *Wood v. Strickland (supra m.v.)*, because they should have known that a lengthy suspension without any type of adjudicative hearing violated procedural due process. Despite these holdings, the district court declined to award damages in the absence of proof of actual injury. The court of appeals reversed and remanded, holding that the students were entitled to recover substantial "non-punitive" damages, even if their suspensions had been justified and even if they did not prove that any

---

*For a case vacated and remanded in light of this decision, see *Smalling v. Epperson*, 438 U.S. 948 (1978).

12

other actual injury, aside from the missed school days, was caused by the denial of due process.

Holding: (7/1x0) In the absence of proof of actual injury, students who have been suspended without the requisite procedural due process are entitled to recover only nominal damages.

Basis: The basic purpose of a § 1981 damages award should be to compensate persons for injuries incurred by the denial of constitutional rights. This traditional tort principle hardly could have been foreign to the members of Congress who enacted this post-Civil War legislation. There is no legislative history to indicate an intent to establish a more formidable deterrent. Although the denial of constitutional rights, other than procedural due process, may require more substantial damage awards than the common law tort rules of damages, that is a separate matter not at issue in this case. Violations of due process do not, as compared to defamation per se, necessarily cause strong feelings of mental and emotional distress. An award of nominal damages recognizes the absolute right to procedural due process even where there is no proof of actual injury.

CANNON v. UNIVERSITY OF CHICAGO, 441 U.S. 677 (1979)

Facts: In this suit the plaintiff sought admission to the medical school at the University of Chicago and alleged that her application was denied because she was a woman. The medical education program at this private university was receiving federal financial assistance at the time her application for admission was denied. She based her original complaint on several federal statutes, but upon appeal the basis of her allegation was limited to Title IX of the Education Amendments of 1972. Both the district court and the court of appeals ruled favorably on the defendant-institution's motion for dismissal, holding that Title IX does not contain an implied private remedy, i.e., an individual right to damages, and concluded that the termination of federal funding was intended as the exclusive remedy for Title IX violations.

Holding: (5/1x3) Title IX contains an implied private cause of action.

Bases: The Court indicated that in cases where the statute is silent or ambiguous about a private remedy, the appropriate test of Congress's intent consists of the four factors identified in *Cort v. Ash,* 422 U.S. 66 (1975):

1) Whether the statute was enacted for the benefit of a special class of which plaintiff is a member? Yes. Title IX specifically confers a benefit on persons discriminated on the basis of sex; and plaintiff is clearly a member of that class.

2) Whether there is any indication of legislative intent to create a private remedy? Yes. The legislative history shows that the drafters of Title IX assumed that it would be interpreted in the same manner as Title VI, which had already been constructed by lower federal courts as creating a private remedy.

3) Whether implication of such a remedy is consistent with the underlying purposes of the statutory scheme? Yes. It will assist in achieving one of the two fundamental purposes of the Act, i.e., providing individual citizens protection against discriminatory practices.

4) Whether the subject matter involves an area not basically of concern to the states? Yes. Since the Civil War, the federal government has been the primary forum for protecting citizens against invidious discrimination.

Although the Court viewed it as far better for Congress to be specific when creating such rights, it found Title IX to present the atypical situation in which all four factors in *Cort v. Ash* are satisfied.

SOUTHEASTERN COMMUNITY COLLEGE v. DAVIS, 442 U.S. 397 (1979)

Facts: Plaintiff suffered from a serious hearing disability. Even with an improved hearing aid she had to rely on lipreading to understand spoken speech. She enrolled in a state community college that receives federal funds. She was denied admission to the college's associate degree nursing program, based on the assessment of the executive director of the state board of nursing, who stated that it would be unsafe for the plaintiff to participate in the regular clinical training program and to practice as a nurse. The executive director concluded that those modifications needed to enable her to participate safely would prevent her from fully realizing the benefits of the program. Upon her request for reconsideration, the college's nursing staff deliberated and again voted to deny her admission. Plaintiff then filed suit in federal court alleging a denial of her Fourteenth Amendment rights and of § 504 of the Rehabilitation Act of 1973. Section 504 prohibits discrimination against an "otherwise qualified handicapped individual" in federally funded programs "solely by reason of his handicap."

Holding: (9x0) The refusal of an educational institution to admit an individual with a severe hearing disability to a nursing program is not violative of § 504 of the Rehabilitation Act.

Basis: Section 504 by its language does not compel educational institutions to disregard the disabilities of handicapped individuals or to make substantial modifications in their programs to allow disabled persons to participate. The HEW regulations reinforce rather than contradict the conclusion that an "otherwise qualified" person is one who is able to meet all of a program's requirements in spite of his handicap.

    Given the present record, it appears likely that the plaintiff could not benefit from any affirmative action that the regulations could reasonably be interpreted as requiring. If the regulations were to require more substantial adjustments, they would constitute an unauthorized extension of the statute.

IV. Employee Rights and Responsibilities

NASHVILLE GAS CO. v. SATTY, 434 U.S. 136 (1977)*

Facts: Pursuant to the defendant's mandatory maternity leave policies, employees disabled by pregnancy do not receive sick pay, while those who are disabled by reason of nonoccupational sickness or injury do. Also, upon return from pregnancy leave employees lose all accumulated job seniority; thus they will only be re-employed in permanent jobs if no other employees apply for the positions. Plaintiff began to work in March 1969 as a clerk, commenced maternity leave in December 1972, gave birth in January 1973, and sought re-employment in March 1973. She obtained only a temporary position, which had a lower rate of pay than she had received previously. The three permanent positions she applied for were awarded to employees who had started work while she was on maternity leave.

Holding: (6½/2½x0) 1) A policy of denying employees returning from pregnancy leave their accumulated seniority violates Title VII of the Civil Rights Act of 1964. 2) A policy of not awarding sick leave pay to pregnant employees is not a violation of Title VII, unless it can be shown to be a mere pretext designed to effect an invidious discrimination against members of one sex.

Basis: 1) On its face the seniority policy is neutral in its treatment of male and female employees. However, it is apparent that the policy had a discriminatory effect, imposing on women a substantial burden that men need not suffer. There was no proof of any business necessity to justify this disparate burden.

2) The Court upheld a similar policy in *General Electric Co. v. Gilbert,* 429 U.S. 125 (1976), but it recognized there and in

---

*For a case vacated and remanded in light of this decision, see *Richmond Unified School District v. Berg,* 434 U.S. 158 (1977).

Geduldig (supra m.v.) that on its face the neutrality of such a policy would not suffice if it can be shown to be a pretext for sex discrimination.

UNITED STATES v. SOUTH CAROLINA, 445 F. Supp 1094 (D.S.C. 1977), *aff'd,* 434 U.S. 1026 (1978)

Facts: For over 30 years the state of South Carolina and its agencies have used scores on the National Teacher Examinations (NTE) to make decisions with respect to the certification of teachers and the amount of state aid payable to local school districts. Local school boards within the state have used scores on the NTE for selection and compensation of teachers. The United States Attorney General filed suit against the state, three of its agencies, and the local school boards in the state, challenging as racially discriminatory the use of NTE scores for certification as well as salary purposes. The National Education Association and other groups and individuals subsequently sued for essentially the same relief and later became plaintiff intervenors in this same action.

Decision: Summarily affirmed (7x2)

Holding: (of the lower court) The governmental use of minimum score requirements on the NTE for both certification purposes and as a factor in determining teacher salaries is not a violation of the equal protection clause of the Fourteenth Amendment nor a violation of Title VII.

Basis: (of the lower court's decision) Plaintiff failed to prove discriminatory intent, as required by *Washington v. Davis (supra m.v.)* for equal protection claims, especially with regard to the recently revised use of the test. In the absence of such proof, the "rational relationship" standard applies. The state's use of the NTE for both certification and pay purposes meets this standard, because it is a valid, reliable, and economical means for measuring one element of effective teaching: the degree of knowledge possessed by the teacher.

Plaintiffs proved that the use of the NTE score had a substantially disproportionate impact on blacks, thus shifting the burden of justifying use of NTE to the defendants. The defendants met their burden through an extensive validity study conducted by Educational Testing Service, the test's publisher. Given that the only alternative offered by the plaintiffs was graduation from an approved teacher education program, the use of the test survives the "business necessity" test of *Griggs v. Duke Power Co. (supra m.v.).*

LOS ANGELES v. MANHART, 435 U.S. 702 (1978)

Facts: Based on a study of mortality tables and its own experience, the Los Angeles Department of Water and Power determined that its female employees would, as a class, outlive its male employees. As a result, it required female employees to make significantly larger pension fund contributions than their male counterparts, thus causing a differential in take-home pay. A class action suit was brought to seek an injunction and restitution. While the action was pending, California enacted a law prohibiting certain municipal agencies from requiring higher pension fund contributions from female employees. The Department amended its plan accordingly.

Holding: (4/2½x1½) A pension plan that requires larger contributions from female employees than male employees is a violation of Title VII. Retroactive relief in such cases is available only under certain circumstances.

Basis: Citing the language and purpose of Title VII, the Court reasoned that the existence or nonexistence of sex discrimination is to be determined by comparison of individual, not class, characteristics. The Court also concluded that one senator's isolated comment on the Senate floor cannot change the effect of the plain language of the Bennett Amendment, which allowed compensation differentials based on sex that had been authorized by the four specific exceptions in the Equal Pay Act of 1963. The meshing of the decision with *General Electric Co. v. Gilbert,* 429 U.S. 125 (1976) and *Geduldig (supra)* was achieved by the Court only with great difficulty, as reflected in the split votes.

BOARD OF TRUSTEES OF KEENE STATE COLLEGE v. SWEENEY, 439 U.S. 24 (1978), *vacating* 569 F. 2d 169 (1st Cir. 1978)

Facts: Dr. Christine Sweeney was first appointed to the Department of Education faculty at Keene State College in 1969. In 1972 she was granted tenure. In 1973 she sought promotion to the rank of full professor. Although her department head recommended in favor of the promotion, the faculty's Evaluation Advisory Committee voted not to grant the promotion and its decision was upheld by the Faculty Appeals Committee. She initiated the process again, and was turned down. After the faculty appeals process produced no findings of erroneous or biased treatment, the college president initiated his own inquiry into the matter. He found no evidence of sex discrimination. The following year she was elevated to the rank of full professor. Dr. Sweeney had sought relief from the Equal Employment Opportunity Commission (EEOC) after her second unsuccessful attempt. Inasmuch as this case involved disparate treatment rather than disparate impact, the district court properly identified the burden-shifting analysis of the *Furnco* and *McDonnell Douglas* decisions (see "Basis" below) as the appropriate framework. Expressly refusing to follow the doctrine of judicial deference for the academic process, the court of appeals held that the defendant-institution had failed to rebut the prima facie case because it failed to prove the absence of a discriminatory motive.

Holding: (5x4) In Title VII employment discrimination cases, the employer need only articulate some legitimate, nondiscriminatory reason for the employee's rejection; it need not prove absence of discriminatory motive.

Basis: As outlined in *McDonnell Douglas Corp. v. Green,* 411 U.S. 792 (1973) and refined in *Furnco Construction Corp. v. Waters,* 438 U.S. 567 (1978), this Court developed a three-step process for Title VII trials: 1) plaintiff bears the initial burden of establishing a prima facie case of employment discrimination; 2) the burden shifts to the defendant to rebut the prima facie case by showing that a legitimate, nondiscriminatory reason accounted for its actions; and 3) if the rebuttal is successful, the burden shifts back to the plaintiff to show that the stated reason was a mere pretext for discrimination. The court of appeals used two contradictory standards for the second step, implying that they were interchangeable. The latter standard—proving the absence of a discriminatory motive—would make the third step in the *Furnco* and *McDonnell Douglas* analysis superfluous.

GIVHAN v. WESTERN LINE CONSOLIDATED SCHOOL DISTRICT, 439 U.S. 410 (1979)

Facts: Plaintiff was a black teacher in a school district under a desegregation order. At the end of the 1970-71 school year, her contract was not renewed based on several reasons, including manifestations of an antagonistic attitude. Plaintiff filed a complaint intervening in a desegregation suit and sought reinstatement on First Amendment grounds and on another basis not at issue herein. In an effort to show that its decision was justified, the defendant-school district introduced evidence of, among other things, a series of private encounters between the plaintiff and the principal, in which she allegedly made petty and unreasonable demands in a manner described by the principal as "insulting," "loud," and "arrogant." The district court found that the primary reason for the school board's failure to renew her contract was her criticism of the policies and practices of the school district.

Holding: (9x0) If a teacher is dismissed primarily based on her private expression of criticism to her principal of school board policies and practices, she is entitled to reinstatement if she would have been rehired but for her criticism.

Basis: The court's decisions in *Pickering, Perry,* and *Mount Healthy* (all *supra m.v.*) do not support the conclusion that a public employee forfeits his protection against governmental abridgment of freedom of expression if he decides to express his views privately rather than publicly. While these cases each arose in the context of a public employee's public expression, the rule to be derived from them is not dependent on that largely coincidental fact. Nor is the "captive audience" rationale, applicable; having opened his office door to the plaintiff-teacher, the principal was hardly in a position to argue that he was the unwilling recipient of her views. Since this case was tried before *Mount Healthy* (*supra m.v.*) was decided, the case is remanded for further proceedings under its "but for" test. *Mount Healthy* held that if a teacher can show his First Amendment rights were violated by a school board's dismissal of him, the school board can, nevertheless, justify its dismissal if it can show it would have dismissed him anyway for independent reasons. Thus, he must show he should still be employed *but for* First Amendment violations.

HARRAH INDEPENDENT SCHOOL DISTRICT v. MARTIN, 440 U.S. 194 (1979)

Facts: Plaintiff was a tenured teacher in Oklahoma. One of the regulations in her contract required teachers holding only a bachelor's degree to earn five semester hours of college credit every three years. Under the terms of this continuing education regulation, noncompliance was sanctioned by withholding salary raises. Plaintiff persistently refused to comply with such regulations, resulting in the forfeiture of salary increases in the 1972-74 school years. After her contract had been renewed for 1973-74, the Oklahoma legislature enacted a law mandating certain salary raises for teachers regardless of their compliance with continuing education requirements. The school board, thus deprived of its previous method of sanction, notified plaintiff that it would not renew her contract for the 1974-75 school year unless she completed five semester hours by April 10, 1974. She refused to comply, and after notice and a hearing the board voted at the April 1974 meeting not to renew her contract for the following year based on the statutorily specified grounds of "*willful* neglect of duty."

Holding: (8/1x0) A school board's prospective rule establishing contract nonrenewal as the sanction for not complying with a continuing education requirement is constitutional.

Bases: A claim of a denial of substantive due process under these circumstances is wholly untenable because 1) plaintiff's interest is not anything like the personal matters of procreation, marriage, and family life involved in prior due process cases affirmatively decided by this Court, and 2) the board's rule was reasonably established and effectuated.

A reliance upon the equal protection clause is likewise not valid because 1) plaintiff has not asserted a suspect classification or fundamental right, and 2) the board's continuing education rule is rationally related to the legitimate concern about the educational qualifications of its teachers. Imposition of the new sanction admittedly placed plaintiff and three other teachers in a class different from those teachers who had previously complied, but any sanction designed to enforce compliance with a valid rule falls only on those who break the rule. The constitutional test for such a sanction is not the willingness of those governed by the rule to accept the consequences of noncompliance.

AMBACH v. NORWICK, 441 U.S. 68 (1979)

Facts: Two unsuccessful applicants for teaching certification in New York State sued to enjoin enforcement of a New York statute that forbids aliens from obtaining public school teacher certification. Both plaintiffs were married to U.S. citizens, had been in this country for over 10 years, and had earned admirable academic records at U.S. colleges. The New York statute con-

	tained exceptions, including where the Commissioner of Education determines a special need for the person's skills or competencies.

Holding: (5x4) A statute that generally prohibits, with some exceptions, aliens from obtaining teacher certification is constitutional.

Basis: The Court's general limitation of statutory exclusions of aliens is less strict in the area of public employment, specifically for functions that go to the heart of representative government. Thus, rather than the strict scrutiny with which the government generally views classifications based on alienage, such public interest exclusions are accorded a relaxed standard, wherein the employer need show only a rational relationship to a legitimate governmental interest rather than a compelling justification. The role of public education, and the degree of responsibility and discretion teachers possess in fulfilling that role, support the conclusion that public school teachers come well within the "governmental function" principle recognized in previous Supreme Court decisions. The citizenship requirement for a teaching certificate bears a rational relationship to the legitimate state interest in public education, for the people of New York, acting through their legislature, have made a judgment that, generally, persons who are citizens are better qualified than those who have rejected the open invitation to commit their primary duty and loyalty to this country.

UNITED STEELWORKERS v. WEBER, 443 U.S. 193 (1979)

Facts: A collective bargaining agreement entered into between a union and a corporation contained an affirmative action plan to eliminate conspicuous racial imbalances in the corporation's almost exclusively white craft work force. At one plant where the craft work force was less than 2% black, even though the local work force was 39% black, the corporation established a training program and selected trainees on the basis of seniority, with the proviso that at least 50% of the new trainees were to be black until the aforementioned percentages reached an approximate balance. During the first year of the plan, the most junior black trainee selected had less seniority than several white production workers who had been rejected from the program. One such white worker instituted a class action suit in federal court, alleging that the plan's selection system violated Title VII of the Civil Rights Act of 1964.

Holding: (5x2) A private corporation's voluntary affirmative action plan, granting, through an agreement with the union, preference to black employees over more senior white employees for admission to training programs for traditionally segregated job categories, is not violative of Title VII.

Basis: Emphasizing the narrowness of its inquiry to voluntary and private sector affirmative action plans, the Court reasoned that a literal interpretation of Title VII would result in practices completely at variance with the purpose of the statute. It cited legislative history in support of the broad purposes of the statute.

GOMEZ v. TOLEDO, 446 U.S. 635 (1980)

Facts: Plaintiff had been a detective in the Puerto Rican police since 1968. In 1975 he submitted a sworn statement to his supervisor that two other detectives had offered false evidence in a criminal case under their investigation. As a result, he was transferred to a noninvestigative position. The police department's legal division investigated the matter, concluding that his factual allegations were true. A year later he was subpoenaed to testify as a defense witness in a criminal case arising out of the evidence he had alleged to be false. He was subsequently brought up on criminal charges, based on evidence furnished by the police department, for the alleged unlawful wiretapping of the two other detectives' telephones. The police department suspended him the following month, and two months later discharged him without a hearing. He was subsequently exonerated in the courts of Puerto Rico. He then sought review of his discharge, which after a hearing, was revoked, and the police department was ordered to reinstate him with back pay. He then filed a § 1983 suit in federal court for damages, contending that his discharge violated his procedural due process rights. The district court dismissed his complaint, and the court of appeals affirmed, adding that plaintiff had failed to plead as part of his claim that the defendant had committed the alleged act in bad faith.

Holding: (8/1x0) In a § 1983 action, the good faith element of the qualified immunity is a required part of the public official's defense, not of the plaintiff's claim.

Basis: In *Owen (supra)*, the court pointed out that as remedial legislation, § 1983 is to be construed generously to further its primary purpose of vindicating constitutional guarantees. In

Wood v. Strickland (*supra m.v.*) and in other cases, the Court accommodated common law tradition and strong public policy reasons by according public officials a qualified immunity from damages liability for acts done on the basis of an objectively reasonable belief that those acts were lawful. As the Court's decisions make clear, the qualified immunity is a defense, based on facts particularly within the knowledge and control of the defendant-public official.

DELAWARE STATE COLLEGE v. RICKS, 449 U.S. 250 (1980)

Facts: Plaintiff, a black from Liberia, in 1970 became a member of the faculty at Delaware State College, a state institution attended predominantly by blacks. In February 1973 the college's Tenure Committee recommended that he not receive a tenured position in the Education Department. The Committee agreed to reconsider its position the following year, and in February 1974 it confirmed the earlier recommendation. In March 1974 the board of trustees voted to deny him tenure. Plaintiff immediately filed a grievance alleging national origin discrimination. The board, per its policies, sent him official notice in June 1974 of its decision and offered him a one-year "terminal" contract. Soon after the grievance committee voted to recommend denial of his grievance. Plaintiff signed the contract without objection or reservations in September 1974, and a week later the board notified him that it had denied his grievance. In April 1974 he had filed an employment discrimination charge with the Equal Employment Opportunity Commission (EEOC), which it accepted later that month after obtaining a jurisdictional waiver from the state fair employment practices agency. More than two years later the EEOC issued a "right to sue letter." Plaintiff filed this lawsuit in September 1977 based on Title VII and 42 U.S.C. § 1981. The college moved to dismiss both claims as untimely, arguing that their applicable time limits (180 days and 4 years, respectively) began to run when the board officially notified him of the decision to deny him tenure and to offer him a one-year terminal contract.

Holding: (5x4) The filing limitation periods of Title VII and § 1981 commence at the time of the alleged discriminatory acts, not when the consequences of the acts culminate. In this case the periods commenced with official notification of the board's decision of denial of tenure not with the subsequent notification of the decision of denial of grievance nor the subsequent expiration of the terminal contract.

Basis: Mere continuity of employment is insufficient to prolong the life of a cause of action for employment discrimination. If plaintiff intended to complain of a discriminatory charge, he should have identified the alleged discriminatory acts that continued until, or occurred at the time of, the actual termination of his employment. The Court cited some of its previous decisions and those of the Ninth Circuit to support its reasoning.

EQUAL EMPLOYMENT OPPORTUNITY COMMISSION v. ASSOCIATED DRY GOODS CORPORATION, 499 U.S. 590 (1981)

Facts: Title VII of the Civil Rights Act of 1964 limits the authority of the Equal Employment Opportunity Commission (EEOC) to make public disclosure of information that it has obtained in investigating and attempting to resolve a claim of employment discrimination. Seven employees of a department store chain filed complaints of employment discrimination with the EEOC. The EEOC began its investigation by requesting the company to provide employment records of the complainants and statistics and other information relating to the company's general personnel policies. The company refused to provide the information unless the EEOC agreed beforehand not to disclose any of the requested material to the charging parties. After the EEOC subpoenaed the material, the company filed this suit to enjoin enforcement of the subpoena.

Holding: (5/½x1½) Congress did not include charging parties with the right to determine to whom disclosure of confidential information is legal under Title VII, but charging parties are entitled only to the information in their own files, not in those of other employees.

Basis: The language, logic, scheme, and legislative history of the disclosure provisions support this ruling. Administrative convenience cannot override the prohibitions of the statute.

TEXAS DEPARTMENT OF COMMUNITY AFFAIRS v. BURDINE, 101 S. Ct. 1089 (1981)

Facts: Plaintiff was hired by the Texas Department of Community Affairs in January 1968 as an accounting clerk. She was promoted in July 1972 to the position of field services coordinator. Her division director resigned in November of that year and plaintiff was assigned additional duties. She applied for the director's position, but it remained vacant for six months. After being pressured by its federal funding agency to fill said position, the department hired a male from another division in the agency. In reducing staff to improve efficiency, he fired plaintiff and two other employees, retaining one male as the only remaining professional employee in the division. Plaintiff was soon rehired by the department and assigned to another division, where she received salary and promotions commensurate with what she would have received had she been appointed to the director's position in her former division. She filed suit in federal court, alleging the failure to promote and the subsequent decision to terminate her had been predicated on sex discrimination in violation of Title VII. The district held that neither decision was based on gender discrimination. The court of appeals reversed in part, holding that in order to rebut plaintiff's prima facie case of gender discrimination, the defendant in a Title VII case bears the burden of proving by a preponderance of the evidence that 1) there were legitimate, nondiscriminatory reasons for the employment action, and 2) those hired or promoted were objectively better qualified than the plaintiff.

Holding: (9x0) In the second step of a Title VII case, the burden of production, not persuasion, shifts to the defendant to present admissible evidence of a legitimate, nondiscriminatory reason for his decision.

Basis: The court of appeals misconstrued the nature of the burden that *McDonnell Douglas* and its progeny (see *Sweeney supra*) place on the defendant. It improperly placed the burden of persuasion on the defendant apparently because it feared that under the lesser standard the employer could compose fictitious legitimate reasons for his actions. The fear is unwarranted because 1) the defendant's explanation of its legitimate reasons must be clear and reasonably specific; 2) the defendant retains an incentive to persuade the trier of fact that the employment decision was valid, and 3) the liberal discovery rules in federal court are supplemented in a Title VII suit by the plaintiff's access to EEOC investigatory files concerning her complaint (see *EEOC v. Associated Dry Goods supra*). Its second rule would require an employer to give preferential treatment to minorities or women, whereas Title VII demands neutrality, leaving the discretion to the employer to choose among equally qualified candidates according to lawful criteria.

NORTHWEST AIRLINES v. TRANSPORT WORKERS UNION, 101 S. Ct. 1571 (1981)

Facts: Continuously from 1947 to 1974, Northwest Airlines paid higher wages to its male cabin attendants, who were classified as pursers, than to its female cabin attendants, who were classified as stewardesses. During that period both the male and female cabin attendants were represented by first one union and then another; and their wages were fixed by collective bargaining agreements. In 1970 one of the female cabin attendants filed a class action against the company, contending that the wage differential violated the Equal Pay Act and Title VII. Finding the two classifications of positions to require equal skill, effort, and responsibility, the district court entered judgment of 20 million dollars to the plaintiff class. The defendant company then brought this action asserting claims of contribution and indemnification against the two unions.

Holding: (8x1) An employer held liable to its female employees for back pay because collectively bargained wage differentials were found to violate the Equal Pay Act of 1963 and Title VII of the Civil Rights Act of 1964 does not have a federal statutory or common-law right to contribution from unions that allegedly bear at least partial responsibility for the statutory violations.

Bases: The *Cort* factors (see *Cannon supra*) do not favor an implied cause of action for contribution under either statute. The power of federal courts to fashion appropriate remedies for unlawful conduct is very limited (e.g., obtaining in admiralty law) and does not extend to comprehensive legislative schemes, which these two statutes are.

COUNTY OF WASHINGTON v. GUNTHER, 101 S. Ct. 2242 (1981)

Facts: Plaintiffs were four women who were employed to guard female prisoners. The County of Washington, Oregon, paid them substantially lower wages than it paid to male guards, who guarded the male prisoners. In January 1974 the county eliminated the female section of the jail, transferred the female prisoners to the jail of a nearby county, and discharged the plaintiffs. They filed suit in federal court seeking back pay and other relief under Title VII. The district court found that the jobs of the male and female guards were not substantially equal; the male guards supervised more than 10 times as many prisoners per guard, while the female guards devoted more of their time to clerical duties. It also held as a matter of law that a sex-based wage discrimination claim cannot be brought under Title VII unless it would satisfy the equal work standard of the Equal Pay Act.

Holding: (5x4) The Bennett Amendment* does not restrict Title VII's prohibition of sex-based wage discrimination to claims of equal pay for equal work.

Basis: The language of the Bennett Amendment suggests, and its legislative history supports, an intention to incorporate only the affirmative defenses of the Equal Pay Act into Title VII. Additional support is found in the remedial purposes of Title VII and the Equal Pay Act.

Plaintiffs did not base their claim and thus the Court did not decide the controversial issue of "comparable worth," under which the intrinsic worth or difficulty of a job is compared with that of other jobs in the same organization or community.

---

*The Bennett Amendment provides: "It shall not be an unlawful employment practice under [Title VII] for any employer to differentiate upon the basis of sex in determining the amount of wages . . . to be paid to employees . . . if such differentiation is authorized by [the Equal Pay Act]."

V. Race, Language, and Sex Discrimination

REGENTS OF THE UNIVERSITY OF CALIFORNIA v. BAKKE, 438 U.S. 265 (1978)

Facts: Plaintiff, a white male, applied to the medical school of the University of California at Davis in 1973 and 1974 and was rejected both times. The medical school had two admissions programs for each year's entering class of 100 students: the regular admission program and the special admissions program. Sixteen of the 100 openings were allocated to the special program, which had somewhat relaxed requirements for minority-group candidates. During 1971-1974, 63 minority students were admitted under the special program and 44 under the regular program. No disadvantaged whites were admitted under the special program, although many applied. In both years that plaintiff was rejected, based on his applications under the regular program, special applicants were admitted with lower scores than his. After his second rejection, he filed suit in state court to compel his admission to Davis' medical school, alleging that the special admission program operated to exclude him on the basis of race in violation of the Fourteenth Amendment's equal protection clause, a provision in the California constitution, and Title VI of the Civil Rights Act of 1964, which provides, among other things, that no person shall on the ground of race or color be excluded from participating in any program receiving federal financial assistance.

Holding: (1/4x4) Race may be used as *a* factor but not *the* factor in university admissions.

Basis: In view of its legislative history, Title VI must be held to proscribe only those racial classifications that would violate the equal protection clause. Whether the special admissions program's allocation is described as a quota or as a goal, it is a line drawn on the basis of race and ethnic status. Racial and ethnic distinctions of any sort are inherently suspect and thus call for strict judicial scrutiny. The medical school's purposes of helping victims of societal discrimination, promoting better healthcare delivery to deprived citizens, and attaining a diverse student body were not shown to be sufficiently compelling in this case to justify foreclosing consideration to persons like the plaintiff.

COLUMBUS BOARD OF EDUCATION v. PENICK, 443 U.S. 449 (1979)*

Facts: A group of students in the Columbus, Ohio, school system brought a class action claiming that cumulative actions of the board of education had the purpose and effect of causing and perpetuating racial segregation in violation of the Fourteenth Amendment. The district court found that 1) at the time of *Brown v. Board of Education* (*supra m.v.*) the board had not been operating a racially neutral unitary school system, but had been operating separate, black schools in one area of the city as a direct result of intentional acts of the board and its administrators, 2) the board had failed to discharge its constitutional obligation to disestablish the dual school system in the interim since 1954, and 3) that since 1954 the board's actions and practices had aggravated rather than alleviated racially identifiable schools through decisions involving such matters as teacher assignment, attendance zoning, and school site selection. Concluding that at the time of trial the board's intentional segregative acts and omissions violated the Fourteenth Amendment, the district court enjoined continuing discrimination on the basis of race and ordered submission of a systematic desegregation plan.

Holding: (5/2x2) Local board actions such as teacher assignment, attendance zoning, and school site selection can constitute sufficient proof of discriminatory intent and impact to establish an equal protection violation and to warrant a systematic remedy.

Basis: Based on *Keyes v. School Dist. No. 1, Denver, Colo.* (*supra m.v.*) proof of purposeful and effective maintenance of separate black schools in a substantial part of a school system is itself prima facie proof of a dual school system and absent sufficient contrary proof supports a systematic remedy.

---

*Rehearing denied, 444 U.S. 887 (1979)

DAYTON BOARD OF EDUCATION v. BRINKMAN ("DAYTON II"), 443 U.S. 526 (1979)

Facts: After the Court had vacated the lower courts' order of a systemwide remedy in *Dayton I (supra m.v.)*, the district court held a supplementary evidentiary hearing. Based on a review of the entire record, the district court found that although there had been various instances of purposeful segregation in the past, the plaintiffs had failed to prove that these acts had any current incremental segregative effects. The court of appeals reversed the district court's dismissal, holding that the consequences of Dayton's dual system in combination with the intentionally segregative impact of its various past practices constituted an appropriate basis for a systemwide remedy.

Holding: (5x4) In order to establish a sufficient case of current systemwide segregation and thus the appropriateness of a systemwide remedy, plaintiffs need only show the school board's failure to fulfill its affirmative duty to disestablish its dual system; they need not prove with respect to each subsequent act of discrimination its individual effect on current patterns of segregation.

Basis: The Court cited *Wright, Davis,* and *Keyes (all supra m.v.)* in reasoning that the measure of the post-*Brown I (supra m.v.)* conduct of a school board that had operated a systemwide dual program in 1954 is the effectiveness, not the purpose, of its actions in decreasing or increasing the segregation caused by the dual system. The Court cited *Keyes* and *Columbus (supra)* to support 1) the heavy burden of a school board found to be in violation of *Brown,* and 2) the inferential connection between substantial and systemwide discrimination.

BOARD OF EDUCATION OF THE CITY OF NEW YORK v. HARRIS, 444 U.S. 130 (1979)

Facts: The New York City Board of Education sued to enjoin HEW to fund its 3.5 million dollar ESAA application, which had been given a favorable ranking but was denied funding based on the Act's eligibility requirements. The 1972 Emergency School Aid Act provides funds to encourage the voluntary elimination, reduction, or prevention of minority group isolation in elementary and public schools. The Act declares an education agency ineligible if, after the date of the Act, 1) "it had in effect any practice which results in the disproportionate de-motion or dismissal of instructional or other personnel from minority groups," or 2) "otherwise engages in discrimination . . . in the hiring, promotion, or assignment of employees." HEW found the board ineligible based upon statistical evidence showing a pattern of racially disproportionate assignments of minority teachers in relation to the number of minority students at the respective schools. The board claimed that the racially disproportionate teacher assignments resulted from compliance with state law, provisions of collective bargaining agreements, licensing requirements for particular teaching positions, demographic changes in student population, and the *Aspira* bilingual instruction consent decree. The district court concluded that HEW should have considered these proffered justifications for the statistical disparities and remanded the case to HEW for further consideration. On remand, HEW found that such justifications did not adequately rebut the prima facie evidence of discrimination established by the statutes.

Holding: (5x4) The HEW regulations, which pursuant to the Emergency School Aid Act, call for the withholding of funds based on evidence of disparate impact (without evidence of intentional discrimination) for both standards of the Act's ineligibility provision, are consistent with the Act.

Bases: The overall structure of the Act, Congress's statements of purpose and policy, the legislative history, and the text of the Act's ineligibility provision all point in the direction of the impact test. Although the language of the ineligibility provision is ambiguous, the underlying philosophy of the Act is to reach *de facto* as well as *de jure* segregation via an enticement approach. If there is a distinction between the two standards of the ineligibility provision, there is an irrebuttable presumption of a disparate impact standard for the first standard and a less strict rebuttable disparate impact standard for the second standard. In the latter situation, herein at issue, the burden is on the party against whom the statistical case has been made. That burden could perhaps be carried by proof of "educational necessity," analogous to the "business necessity" defense under Title VII.

A ruling of ineligibility does not make the children who attend New York City schools any worse off. The funds competed for are not wasted for they are utilized to benefit other similarly disadvantaged children. Thus, the Court concluded: "It is a matter of benefits, not of deprivation, and it is a matter of selectivity."

The appropriate standard for Title VI is, in the absence of legislative language that the two Acts are coextensive, a separate matter.

ARMOUR v. NIX, No. 16708 (N.D. Ga. Sept. 24 1979), *aff'd*, 446 U.S. 930 (1980)

Facts: A group of indigent black parents of children who attended metropolitan Atlanta schools filed a class action in 1973, alleging unconstitutional segregation and seeking an interdistrict remedy.

Decision: Summarily affirmed (5x3)

Holding: (of the lower court) Where the vestiges of racial segregation are *de minimus* or only intradistrict, an interdistrict remedy will not be ordered.

Basis: (of the lower court's decision) The relevant test for school desegregation cases in which plaintiffs seek an interdistrict remedy was established in *Milliken I (supra m.v.)* and emphasized in *Dayton II (supra m.v.)*. While a history of *de jure* segregation is relevant to the question of intent, the *Pasadena* decision (*supra m.v.*) established that once the system is unitary or under court order, evidence of subjective intent is required. Historically, official acts of governmental officials at all levels contributed to racial segregation in schooling and housing in the Atlanta area, but public education is currently free from any policy of segregation, and present-day housing patterns are not caused by governmental discrimination.

VI. Procedural Parameters

UNIVERSITY OF TEXAS v. CAMENISCH, 101 S. Ct. 1830 (1981)

Facts: A deaf graduate student at the University of Texas filed a complaint in federal district court, alleging that the university had violated § 504 of the Rehabilitation Act of 1973 by discriminatorily refusing to pay for a sign-language interpreter for him. Section 504 provides that "no otherwise qualified handicapped individual . . . shall, solely by reason of his handicap, be excluded from participation in, be denied the benefits of, or be subjected to discrimination under any program or activity receiving financial assistance." Finding a possibility that the plaintiff would be irreparably harmed in the absence of an injunction and that he was likely to prevail on the merits, the district court granted a preliminary injunction on condition that he post a security bond pending the outcome of the litigation. The court of appeals affirmed. Meanwhile, the university had obeyed the lower court's injunction by paying for his interpreter, and he graduated.

Holding: (8/1x0) Where the terms of a preliminary injunction have been fully and irrevocably carried out, the question of whether it should have been issued is moot, but the question of damages—as preserved by the injunction bond—should be remanded for a trial on the merits.

Basis: The issues of whether the preliminary injunction should have been granted and whether the university should ultimately bear the cost of the interpreter are significantly different and thus separable matters. Preliminary and permanent injunctions are procedurally and substantively not equivalent, since a decision for a preliminary injunction is not tantamount to a decision on the merits. Thus, the first issue is moot but the second issue requires a trial on the merits.

Table of Cases

The principal cases are in italic type. Other cases are in roman type. References are to page number.

*Abington School District v. Schempp. 8
 Ambach v. Norwick, 21
 Armour v. Nix, 33
 Beggans v. Public Funds for Public Schools of New Jersey, 9
 Board of Curators of University of Missouri v. Horowitz, 11
 Board of Education of the City of New York v. Harris, 31
 Board of Trustees of Keene State College v. Sweeney, 18
*Brown v. Board of Education, 30
 Cannon v. University of Chicago, 13
 Carey v. Piphus, 12
 City of Newport v. Fact Concerts, 5
 Columbus Board of Education v. Penick, 30
*Committee for Public Education and Religious Liberty v. Nyquist, 9
 Committee for Public Education v. Regan, 9
 Cort v. Ash, 13, 27
 County of Washington v. Gunther, 27
*Davis v. Board of School Commissioners, 31
 Dayton Board of Education v. Brinkman ("Dayton II"), 31
 Delaware State College v. Ricks, 24
 Equal Employment Opportunity Commission v. Associated Dry Goods Corp., 25
 Furnco Construction Corp. v. Waters, 19
*Geduldig v. Aiello, 18
 General Electric Co. v. Gilbert, 18
 Givhan v. Western Line Consolidated School District, 19
 Gomez v. Toledo, 23
 Harrah Independent School District v. Martin, 20
 Idaho Department of Employment v. Smith, 11

---
*Cases summarized in main volume.

Interim Board of Trustees of Westheimer Independent School District v. Coalition to Preserve Houston, 4
Keyes v. School District No. 1, Denver, Colorado, 30
Kornit v. Board of Education, 1
*Lemon v. Kurtzman ("Lemon I"), 10
*Lemon v. Kurtzman ("Lemon II"), 6, 7
*Levitt v. Commission for Public Education and Religious Liberty, 6, 9
Los Angeles v. Manhart, 18
Maine v. Thiboutot, 3
McDonnell Douglas Corp. v. Green, 19, 26
Milliken v. Bradley ("Milliken I"), 33
Mobile v. Bolden, 2
Monell v. Department of Social Services, 1
Monroe v. Pape, 1
*Mount Healthy City School District v. Doyle, 20
Nashville Gas Co. v. Satty, 16
National Labor Relations Board v. Catholic Bishop of Chicago, 7
New York v. Cathedral Academy, 6
Northwest Airlines v. Transport Workers Union, 27
Owen v. City of Independence, Missouri, 1
Parham v. J.R., vii
*Pasadena City Board of Education v. Spangler, 33
Pennhurst State Hospital v. Halderman, vii
*Perry v. Sindermann, 20
*Pickering v. Board of Education, 20
Regents of the University of California v. Bakke, 29
Richmond Unified School District v. Berg, 16
St. Martin Evangelical Lutheran Church v. South Dakota, 8
Secretary of Public Welfare v. Institutionalized Juveniles, vii
Smalling v. Epperson, 12
Southeastern Community College v. Davis, 14
Stone v. Graham, 7
Texas Department of Community Affairs v. Burdine, 25
United States v. South Carolina, 17
United Steelworkers v. Weber, 22
University of Texas v. Camenisch, 34
*Walz v. Tax Commission, 9
*Washington v. Davis, 17
*Wolman v. Walter, 10
*Wood v. Strickland, 12, 24
Wright v. Council of City of Emporia, 31
Yeshiva University v. NLRB, vii

Index

Admissions, 13, 14, 29
Affirmative action, 22, 29
Alabama, 2
Aliens, 21-22
Attorney General, 4, 17
Attorneys' fees, 3. *See also* Section 1988
Bad faith, 5, 23
Bargaining, collective, 7, 22, 27, 31
Bennett Amendment, 18, 27
Blacks, 2, 19, 24, 30, 33
Burden-shifting, 17, 18-19, 25-26
Business necessity, 16, 17, 32
California, 18
Chicago, 12; University of, 13
Citizenship: *See* Aliens
City council, 1, 5
City manager, 1
Civil Rights Act, 1. *See also* Title VI, Title VII
Class action, 2, 33
Collective bargaining: *See* Bargaining, collective
Common law, 1, 5, 7, 23, 27
Comparable worth, 28
Congress, 3, 7, 13, 25, 31
Constitution: *See* specific Amendments and Freedoms
Damages: compensatory damages, 5; nominal damages, 12-13; punitive damages, 5
Defamation, 13
Desegregation: *See* School districts
Discharge: *See* Dismissal
Dismissal: court, 13, 27; employee, 1, 19, 20, 23, 24; student, 11
Disparate impact, 2, 16, 17, 19, 32
Disparate treatment, 19
Due process: procedural, 12, 12-13, 23; substantive, 20
Elections: *See* Voting
Emergency School Aid Act, 31-32
Equal Employment Opportunity Commission (EEOC), 24, 25
Equal Pay Act, 18, 27, 27-28
Equal Protection, 2, 11, 17, 21, 29, 30. *See also* Fourteenth Amendment

Establishment clause, 7, 9. *See also* First Amendment
Examinations, 9, 11, 17
Excessive entanglement: *See* Three-pronged test
Fifteenth Amendment, 2
First Amendment, 7, 8, 9, 19
Fourteenth Amendment, 2, 11, 12, 14, 17, 29, 30
Freedom of expression, 19. *See also* First Amendment
Freedom of religion, 7. *See also* Establishment clause; First Amendment; Three-pronged test
Governmental function principle, 21
Handicap, discrimination on account of, 14, 34
Hearings, 1, 11, 23
Idaho, 11
Impact: *See* Disparate impact Racial discrimination, purposeful
Kentucky, 7
Leaves, 1, 16. *See also* Pregnancy
Legislative history, 1, 2, 3, 7, 8, 13, 14, 25, 27, 29
Liability: *See* Damages; Public officials; School boards
Liberty interest, 11
Local control, 4. *See also* School boards; School districts
Maine, 3
Maternity: *See* Pregnancy
Mayor, 5
Medical school, 11, 13, 29
Missouri, 1; University of, 11
Municipality: *See* City manager; City Council; Mayor; Public officials; School board; School district
National Education Association, 17
National Labor Relations Act, 7
National Labor Relations Board (NLRB), 7
National origin discrimination, 24
New Jersey, 9
New York, 6, 9, 21

37

Newport jazz festival, 5
Nonpublic schools, 9. *See also* Parochial schools; Religious schools
Notice, 1, 24
Ohio, 9, 30
Oklahoma, 20
Oregon, 27
Parochial schools, 7, 8
Pensions, 18
Police, 1, 23
Pregnancy, 1, 16
Prevailing party, 4
Primary effect: *See* Three-pronged test
Private expression, 19
Property interest, 12
Public official: qualified immunity, 23-24
Public policy, 2, 5, 24
Puerto Rico, 23
Racial discrimination: admissions, 29; desegregation, 19, 30, 31, 32; elections, 2, 4; purposeful, 2, 4, 17, 30, 32, 33; salary and certification, 17
Regulations, HEW, 15, 32
Religious schools, state aid to: reporting services, 9; state-mandated services, 6; test results, 9. *See also* Parochial schools
Respondent superior, 1
Restraining order, 5
School boards; elections, 4; liability, 1, 2, 5; rules, 20. *See also* School districts
School districts: desegregation, 19, 30, 31, 31-32, 33; elections, 4. *See also* School boards

Sectarian schools: *See* Religious schools, state aid to; Three-pronged test
Section 504, 14, 34
Section 1981, 13, 24-25
Section 1983, 1, 2, 3, 5, 23-24
Section 1988, 3
Secular purpose: *See* Three-pronged test
Seniority, 16, 22
Sex discrimination: admissions, 13; maternity leave, 16; promotion, 18, 25; salary, 18, 26, 27; termination, 25, 26
Social Security Act, 3
South Carolina, 17
South Dakota, 9
Teacher certification, 17, 21
Ten Commandments, 7
Tenure, 18, 24
Texas, 4, 25; University of, 34
Three-pronged test: secular purpose, 7, 9; primary effect, 6, 9; excessive entanglement, 6, 9
Time limits, 24
Title VI, 14, 29, 32
Title VII, 16, 17, 18, 22, 24, 25, 25-26, 27, 27-28, 31-32
Title IX, 13
Tort, 13
Unemployment compensation, 8
Voting, 2, 4; Voting Rights Act, 4
Welfare, 3